MALCOLM X

By Barbara M. Linde

Gareth Stevens
Publishing

Please visit our website, www.garethstevens.com. For a free color catalog of all our high-quality books, call toll free 1-800-542-2595 or fax 1-877-542-2596.

Library of Congress Cataloging-in-Publication Data

Linde, Barbara M.
Malcolm X / Barbara M. Linde.
    p. cm. — (Civil rights crusaders)
Includes bibliographical references and index.
ISBN 978-1-4339-5688-1 (pbk.)
ISBN 978-1-4339-5689-8 (6-pack)
ISBN 978-1-4339-5686-7 (library binding)
1. X, Malcolm, 1925-1965—Juvenile literature. 2. Black Muslims—Biography—Juvenile literature. 3. African American Muslims—Biography—Juvenile literature. 4. African American civil rights workers—Biography—Juvenile literature. 5. African Americans—Civil rights—History—20th century—Juvenile literature. 6. African Americans—Biography—Juvenile literature. I. Title.
BP223.Z8L57618 2011
320.54'6092—dc22
[B]

2010054578

First Edition

Published in 2012 by
Gareth Stevens Publishing
111 East 14th Street, Suite 349
New York, NY 10003

Copyright © 2012 Gareth Stevens Publishing

Designer: Katelyn E. Reynolds
Editor: Kristen Rajczak

Photo credits: Cover, pp. 3–24, back cover (background) Shutterstock.com; cover, p. 1 Robert Parent/Time & Life Pictures/ Getty Images; p. 5 Truman Moore/Time & Life Pictures/Getty Images; p. 7 Marion Trikosko, Library of Congress – digital version copyright Science Faction; p. 9 Keystone/Hulton Archive/Getty Images; p. 11 Bob Parent/Hulton Archive/Getty Images; p. 13 Richard Saunders/Hulton Archive/Getty Images; p. 15 Robert L. Haggins/Time & Life Pictures/Getty Images; p. 17 Marvin Lichtner/Time & Life Pictures/Getty Images; p. 19 Express/Hulton Archive/Getty Images.

Printed in the United States of America

CPSIA compliance information: Batch #CS11GS: For further information contact Gareth Stevens, New York, New York at 1-800-542-2595.

CONTENTS

Words in the glossary appear in **bold** type the first time they are used in the text.

CIVIL RIGHTS CRUSADER

Malcolm X spent many years speaking about the importance of **civil rights** for all. At first, he disagreed with other leaders of the civil rights movement about **integration**. He believed in black pride and keeping black people and white people separate. He also disagreed with the idea of bringing about change through peaceful actions. He said blacks needed "freedom, justice, and **equality** by any means necessary." Later experiences changed his mind. He began working with, instead of against, other civil rights leaders. Malcolm X was murdered in 1965, but his work and ideas live on.

Malcolm X was only 39 years old when he died.

▽

5

EARLY LIFE

Malcolm X began life as Malcolm Little. He was born in Nebraska on May 19, 1925. He had seven brothers and sisters. His father, Earl, was a **minister**. His mother, Louise, took care of the family. When Malcolm was about 4, the family moved to Michigan.

Earl Little talked about black pride. He believed blacks would never be treated fairly in the United States. Earl said they could only receive justice by living in Africa. These ideas angered many people. When Malcolm was just 6 years old, Earl died. His family believed Earl's enemies had killed him.

LET FREEDOM RING

When Malcolm was growing up, many places in the United States were **segregated**. African Americans faced **discrimination** in all parts of life.

Malcolm learned many of his early beliefs from his father.

SCHOOL YEARS

After Earl's death, Louise became ill and wasn't able to care for her children. She had to live in a hospital. The children went to live with family members or in **foster homes**. Malcolm lived with a foster family for many years.

Malcolm did well in school. When he was in eighth grade, he told one of his teachers he wanted to become a lawyer. The teacher told Malcolm that black boys couldn't be lawyers. Malcolm became angry. He soon dropped out of school.

LET FREEDOM RING

Malcolm was elected class president when he was a student at Mason Junior High.

Even as a boy, Malcolm believed he would do something important with his life.

▽

PRISON BRINGS CHANGES

As a teenager, Malcolm worked in Boston, Massachusetts, then in New York City. When he moved back to Boston, Malcolm began stealing and selling drugs. In 1946, he went to prison.

While Malcolm was in prison, his brother Reginald told him about the **Nation of Islam** (NOI) and its leader, Elijah Muhammad. Followers were called Black Muslims. They believed that whites kept blacks unequal and that blacks needed a separate state. Malcolm joined the NOI. He changed his last name to "X." In 1952, he got out of prison.

LET FREEDOM RING

Many members of the Nation of Islam used the last name "X." They said their real African names were lost when past family members became slaves.

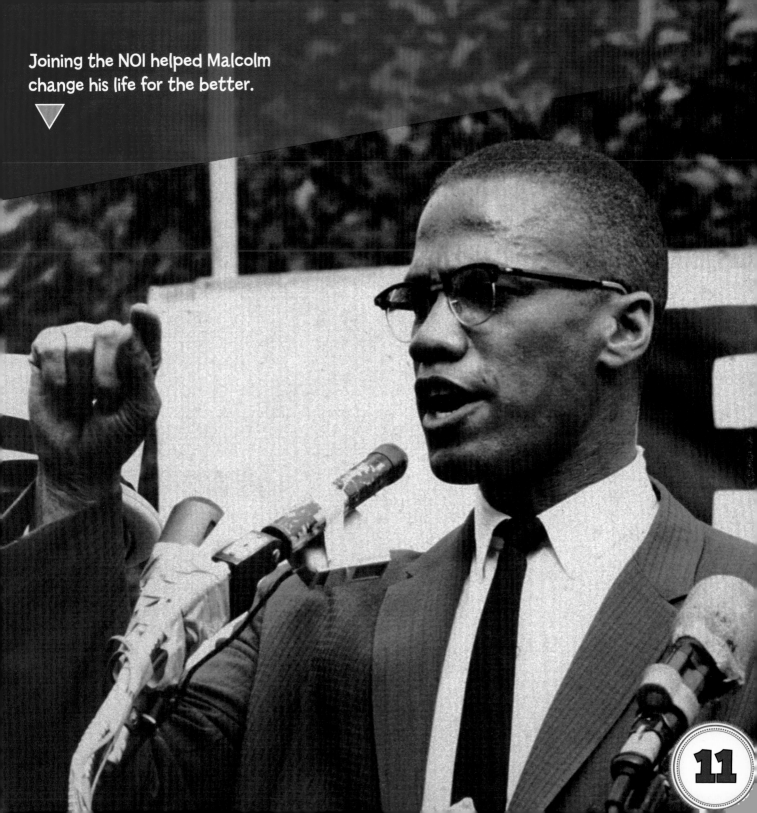

Joining the NOI helped Malcolm change his life for the better.

▽

11

WORKING FOR THE NOI

Malcolm traveled around the country, sharing the NOI's message. He tried to get others to become Black Muslims. Although many people thought the NOI's ideas were hateful, other blacks agreed with those ideas. Malcolm soon became more popular than other leaders of the NOI.

Malcolm discovered that Elijah Muhammad had broken some of the NOI's rules. Malcolm lost trust in him. Elijah tried to stop Malcolm from telling others about his wrongdoing. However, Malcolm wouldn't be quiet.

LET FREEDOM RING

Malcolm gave speeches for the NOI from 1952 to 1963. He was such a wonderful speaker that NOI membership grew from 500 to 30,000 during that time.

Malcolm X speaks to a crowd in Washington, DC, in 1962.

▽

13

CHANGING IDEAS

In 1964, Malcolm left the NOI and formed Muslim Mosque, Inc. This group worked with other civil rights groups.

Malcolm's life changed when he visited the Muslim holy city of Mecca, Saudi Arabia. Malcolm said that he met "blonde-haired, blue-eyed men I could call my brothers." He realized he'd been wrong to think that all whites were evil. Malcolm stopped blaming them for the problems of black people. Instead, he talked about **tolerance** and working together. He changed his name to el-Hajj Malik el-Shabazz.

LET FREEDOM RING

Malcolm married Betty Sanders in 1958. They had six daughters. Betty and the children changed their last name to Shabazz when Malcolm did.

Malcolm holds two of his daughters, Qubilah and Attilah, in 1963.

15

MORE CHANGES, MORE TROUBLES

In 1965, Malcolm started the Organization of Afro-American Unity (OAAU). He wanted the whole world to know about the civil rights problems blacks had in the United States. Malcolm also began speaking about how to improve life for other **minority groups**.

Malcolm disagreed with Elijah and the NOI even more now. He was warned that members of the NOI wanted to kill him. In February 1965, Malcolm's home was set on fire. Malcolm and his family escaped, but the danger wasn't over.

LET FREEDOM RING

Malcolm had to travel with bodyguards to keep him safe from members of the NOI.

After leaving the NOI, Malcolm still traveled all over the United States, spreading his message.

THE END COMES TOO SOON

On February 21, 1965, people filled the Audubon Ballroom in New York City. Everyone waited to hear Malcolm's words. Those words never came. Instead, the people heard loud gunshots. Malcolm X was dead.

Malcolm's wife and their four daughters were there. A few months later, Betty gave birth to twin girls. They never got to meet their father.

More than 1,500 people went to Malcolm's funeral in Harlem. It was also shown on TV.

LET FREEDOM RING

Usually workers dig the grave in which a person is buried. Instead, Malcolm's friends did this sad job themselves.

This photo of Malcolm X was taken just 11 days before his death in 1965.

▽

19

MALCOLM'S WORK LIVES ON

Today, many people know about the life and message of Malcolm X. *The **Autobiography** of Malcolm X* was published in 1965. Malcolm had been working on the book with writer Alex Haley up until his death. In 1992, Spike Lee, a famous movie director, made a movie called *Malcolm X* based on this book. There are also plans to build the Malcolm X Museum in Harlem. There, visitors will be able to see photos of Malcolm X and some of his original papers.

LET FREEDOM RING

Three men from the NOI were charged with Malcolm X's murder. They all went to jail for the crime. The last one got out of prison in 2010.

TIMELINE

1925   Malcolm Little is born on May 19 in Nebraska.

1931   Earl Little, Malcolm's father, dies.

1946   Malcolm goes to prison.

1952   Malcolm changes his last name to X.

1958   Malcolm marries Betty Sanders.

1964   Malcolm leaves the NOI. He starts Muslim Mosque, Inc., and the OAAU.

1965   Malcolm X is murdered on February 21. *The Autobiography of Malcolm X* is published.

GLOSSARY

autobiography: a book someone writes about their life

civil rights: the freedoms granted to US citizens by law

discrimination: treating people differently because of their race or beliefs

equality: being treated the same and given the same freedoms

foster home: a home children go to when their family cannot care for them

integration: opening a group, community, or place to all races

minister: a person who leads a church service

minority group: people who are not part of the main group of people in a society. In the United States, African Americans, Native Americans, and the poor are minority groups.

Nation of Islam: a group that believes in parts of the Islamic faith and in the connection black people have to each other

segregated: the forced separation of races or classes

tolerance: accepting other ideas or points of view

FOR MORE INFORMATION

Books

Gunderson, Jessica. *X: The Biography of Malcolm X*. Mankato, MN: Graphic Library, 2011.

Hardy, Sheila Jackson, and P. Stephen Hardy. *Extraordinary People of the Civil Rights Movement*. New York, NY: Children's Press, 2007.

Websites

African American Odyssey
memory.loc.gov/ammem/aaohtml/exhibit
Watch videos about the history of the civil rights movement. Take a virtual trip through the exhibit at the Library of Congress.

Malcolm X: Make It Plain
www.pbs.org/wgbh/amex/malcolmx
Learn about a film about Malcolm X and see pictures of him.

Malcolm X Official Website
www.malcolmx.com
Read more about Malcolm X's life, look at pictures, and get links to other sites about him.

INDEX